THE VOICE OF A LITERARY FALCON

PAPAI PATRA

Made with ♥ on the Notion Press Platform
www.notionpress.com

TO

MY PROFESSORS

It is my great privilege to dedicate this book to my professors.

Contents

Foreword

It was well to nurture my mind with various poetic works of the twenty-first century's budding poets. But in reading Mr. Patra's poems I treamble like one who gets some shock with the gigantic power of words. I must first explain that I can never forget the moment when he produced his literary thoughts in a jiffy once anonymously but somehow it was revealed to his peers and dissenters. The readers should deal with his language and oeuvre to gratify their grey cells. The different flavour of language is presented here along with different themes. Therefore, I suggest the readers to cast their eyes once at this book. It is hard to put down the book.

Mr. M

21st January, 2023

Preface

Most of the rhetorical language appeared in the poems are nothing but my poetic frenzy. The extreme passion drove me to the unknown region of the literary essence where the dreams are the monarchs of the entire land. Being paralyzed with the literary essence of the poetry of Coleridge, Wordswoth and Keats during my Bachelor's degree, I voluntarily forced myself to compose these poems but with the involuntary passion. I am pretty much sure to articulate that this collection of poetry will give a lot of pleasure to the readers of this century.

THE AUTHOR OF THIS BOOK

21st January, 2023

Acknowledgements

Thanks to the Notion Press publishing house, India. Many thanks to the Poetizier for encouraging me and for making various ittustration for my work at first. And specially thanks to my massive supporters for leading me in this path.

1. Ode to the Soaking Rain

O Rain, feel your dropping tone.
Thy voice raises the sound of marble stone.
The dry Cistern quenched its thirst.
Thine azure figure reveals the Cistern so vast.

Dreaming earth is soaked with thy silvery drops,
Greenery grows in a troaks.
You fulfill the unrequited dream of the earth,
Something is dreary, something is in mirth.

O Rain, from the dozy bed thou awakened the dazzling flowers.
The turf enjoys the trembling showers.
From Summer's igneous surge the earth and air is uplifted.
Thine azure glittering beauty, one lonely cloud has gifted.
Thou soothe the ache of Green leaves.
The chirping birds are soaked, till the drop he gives.
Thou art more temperate like a damsel with her crystalline heart.
Once I saw thy beauteous halo in my glaring heart, heart only.
Rain is gone ere so long.
Poetry of earth to mine ear is the sparkling song.

2. Stopping by the Winter

Snow is falling round the city.
One is thinking about the absurdity.
Everything is looking White.
Animals are taking rest with the Sun's bright.
Hibernation is started between all of them.
To give a rousing shake, one needs to set
the flame.
And lonely as it is, that loneliness
With no expression, nothing to express.
Day is too good, Night is so cold.
The creatures are looking like a garish wrapper's mould.
The Woodchuck takes a great Hibernation
No chance is there, no alternation.
Winter cannot scare me with its empty space.
To scare myself with my own desert place.
Blizzard starts soon after.
My aching heart invites a mitigator.
Ceasing is the favour of Winter.
Call of the wintry bed comes to the mortal ear.

3. An Unknown Painter

Fresco has its own plaster.
Artist can create a short caricature.
Final creation is the new founder.
Some aesthetic comes from here.
Art; a piece of private correspondence.
The depth and passion of its earnest glance.
Nature's glittering beauty goes to the Atelier.
Ethical instruments are ready for the Painter.
Art of storytelling is the privacy of author.
Labour of reading is the readers' favour.
Imagination goes to the zenith's height.
Reflection of this fancy is so bright.
Time reveals everything from it's womb.
There is a stone of invisible tomb.
The painting knows not to blame.
The painter is unknown to his fame.

4. Darkling Pleasure

The dim glimmering moon is shining bright.
But my lacerating heart is not delight.
I cherished to be happy more,
With the pleasant sight at the silvery shore.
But the memories are blurring my sight.
This is the cimmerian night with the gleaming light.
Another day has already passed.
It was the last delight of my lust.
The language of light in darkness is not merely decorative.
Where are the aesthetics of language? Where are they?
Now I wanna explore my life's delight.
As happiness lies within my sight.
Thus making my soul Happy and Delight.
And never turn back the Cimmerian Night.
At this very hour the heavenly voice is so strong and with the saintly song,
I wander wearily through the forest bare in the midnight air, too strong.
I meet with the heather of the moor, their heart is in their mouth again.
Every attempt to mingle myself with the objects of nature is a vain.
Should I do something well or worse ?
The self mine is other and remorse.

5. The Mannlicher in the Manhattan

Listen!
It's not too late, we can go together.
The womb of time has left us without any danger.
See! it's like a particle, squeezed in the dead cell.
Now I become the electron, trying to find out the ladder between the Heaven and Hell.
The ladder we find together.
But the call of the wintry bed comes to one's ear.
Another begins to live in the Manhattan.
But who knows about the imminent danger.
A cozy shelter invites the precious to the Manhattan.
It grows dark, owl screeches, a gusty wind blows over the west edge of Manhattan.
It was a wuthering day indeed.
No sound was detected except the music of nature.
Boom ! Boom! ..... a sudden sound appeared.
No...it was of course the sound of a Mannlicher.
Alas! the moon-shaped corporeal-frame now becomes cold.
That horrific sound didn't tell the truth.
But it was a Mannlicher in the Manhattan for sure.

6. The Falcon

Like most birds,
I chirp,
Like others,
I fly.
This is not an old story that I try.
But the touch of azure-grey wings, dark brown backs, a buff colored underside with brown spots, and white faces with a black tear stripe on the cheeks made me an alien.
The hooked beaks and strong talons made me a raptor.
I become a bird of prey.
I'm alienated.
I counsel myself.
What remains ?
Only a myth and wildlife !
It might be smoother.
I have no mind yet.
But nobody can deny my speed.
Nobody can challenge my aerodynamic torsos and specially pointed wings.
No birds can spend their days with me except my prey.
I'm the fastest, spiritually subsisted and morally persisted.
Seeing my aggressive gesture, the birds become grey.
The gusty wind is my friend.
It's matter of pride to comprehend.
The lustrous eyes of the universe behold my shape.
But my preys !
They gape.

Like lightning or thunder, I fall on the field from the zenith's height and create the bar.
Often I win or I fail.
Indeed, it's a Falcon's life that becomes hell.

7. Heart of Spring

Passion of spring is Nature's ring.
Nature poets are enjoying the joy of Spring.
Enjoys the air it breathes.
The Dandelion of Spring hath its end.
Ode oft wrote about Spring,
Sense of joy may Blossom Blight bring.
Cuckoo is the harbinger of this season.
Soundless roaming, sweet-song creates the reason.
Cherish the Green on the solitary fields.
It reminds, the Summer is just around the corner.
It started to blow in the last Winter.
Now growing to get the summer; it hath short lease.
The blossom bowed down with its one while March is scarcely here.
Is it not difficult to glorify the time on the same year ?

8. Horrific Station

Mild is thy brain, having the hellish fire.
Where thou get the very mingling stir?
Is it infernal in its nature?
Should thou be that shabby creature?
Questions are left with a very weary yearn.
The mild creature is here to emancipate the turn.
Stirring station is not enlightened with the civilized light.
Hellish fire is there but not so bright.
Visible fears are bright but those invisibles are more brighter.
Horrified workshops are now pervaded with the unconscious sensation.
Eternal, infernal fire is existed only in the 'Horrific Station '.

9. Crossing the Seashore

Standing on the vast seashore of Lethe,
I am sipping the sweet breeze of the restless sea.
My feet touch the ancient mossy hills.
An unknown sonorous sound comes to my brimming ear.
The mingling heart stops the oscillation before the bar.
A deep sensation lingers there.
For my bouncing heart the door to freedom is ajar.
Suddenly the cold, unrivaled splash of the oceanic beauty soaks my dappled face.
Such a touch my face never felt before.
The paradise of summer-beauty is only the lonely seashore.
Cadency of the oysters comes to the shore together.
The halo of the unknown region forms the familiar world.
Familiar yet unfortunate.
The moment sharply turns its face to the east.
The Volcanic beauty appears in each corner of the sky.
The Oceanic beauty then hails the Volcanic one.
Till now the splashes spatter on my face.
Now long waiting becomes pregnant with the dawn at seashore.

10. The Final Sight

The Last Shade of the last hour is evaporated.
One tremulous voice was approaching to my brimming ear.
It wasn't the voice of the Volcano or the last shade, Not the voice of the mountain stream.
My ear wanted to abscond.
That boom forced it to be dislocated.
But my mind recognised the great human cry.
Dirty desires of the millions were unsheathed.
Only my austere eyes could catch the final sight of the last shade.
The bucolic station was finding its revolving fate. Every attempt was the spear of the white tongue. But the primitive station was ostracized.
The sword of revolt hit on the throat of humanity. Only the Reeds on the field were shivering.
Was it my final sight or not?

Thank You

Thanks to all the readers from the bottom of my heart. Stay tuned with thy readership, leadership wilt enlighten thy values and ethics.

9 798889 860167

Printed by Libri Plureos GmbH in Hamburg,
Germany